MAKERS OF THE MIDDLE AGES AND RENAISSANCE

Thomas More
and His Struggles of Conscience

Samuel Willard Crompton

CHELSEA HOUSE
PUBLISHERS
A Haights Cross Communications ✦ Company ®

Philadelphia

COVER: Portrait of Sir Thomas More.

CHELSEA HOUSE PUBLISHERS
VP, NEW PRODUCT DEVELOPMENT Sally Cheney
DIRECTOR OF PRODUCTION Kim Shinners
CREATIVE MANAGER Takeshi Takahashi
MANUFACTURING MANAGER Diann Grasse

Staff for Thomas More
EXECUTIVE EDITOR Lee Marcott
EDITORIAL ASSISTANT Carla Greenberg
PRODUCTION EDITOR Noelle Nardone
COVER AND INTERIOR DESIGNER Keith Trego
LAYOUT 21st Century Publishing and Communications, Inc.

© 2006 by Chelsea House Publishers,
a subsidiary of Haights Cross Communications.
All rights reserved. Printed and bound in China.

A Haights Cross Communications ✦ Company ®

www.chelseahouse.com

First Printing

9 8 7 6 5 4 3 2 1

Library of Congress Cataloging-in-Publication Data

Crompton, Samuel Willard.
   Thomas More and his struggles of conscience/Samuel Willard Crompton.
      p. cm.–(Makers of the Middle Ages and Renaissance)
   Includes bibliographical references and index.
   ISBN 0-7910-8636-4
  1. More, Thomas, Sir, Saint, 1478–1535–Juvenile literature. 2. Henry VIII,
King of England, 1491–1547–Relations with humanists–Juvenile literature.
3. Great Britain–History–Henry VIII, 1509–1547–Juvenile literature.
4. England–Intellectual life–16th century–Juvenile literature. 5. Christian
martyrs–England–Biography–Juvenile literature. 6. Statesmen–Great
Britain–Biography–Juvenile literature. 7. Humanists–England–Biography–
Juvenile literature. I. Title. II. Series.
   DA334.M8C86 2005
   942.05'2'092–DC22
                                                                2005003271

Thomas More

and His Struggles of Conscience

CONTENTS

A Family Portrait

Thomas More is one of the most recognizable figures from the sixteenth century. Famous for his public service, his published works, and his martyrdom, he was made a saint of the Catholic Church in 1935, some 400 years after his death. We will look at an artist's sketch of Thomas More and his family to get a better idea of what More might have been like around the age of 50. Every picture tells a story. In fact, an old saying claims that every picture is worth a thousand words. With this in mind, we will use a family portrait from the time of Thomas More to get a better idea of what More and his family were like.

Sometime around 1527 or 1528—historians are not sure of the exact date—a German painter named Hans Holbein came to Thomas More's home in Chelsea, just outside the city of London. Hans Holbein was already a famous painter in Germany, but he was about to become equally famous in England. Years later, he would paint what is still considered the best portrait ever done of King Henry VIII. For now, however, Hans Holbein was just beginning to develop his reputation in England. He had come to Chelsea to paint not only Thomas More, but also More's entire family. Holbein's painting was lost, but a preliminary sketch of More and his family remains today.

Let's start by looking at the extreme left side of the sketch on the next page. We see a woman holding a book. She is Elizabeth Dauncy, one of Thomas More's daughters. She was about 21 when the

A family portrait can provide a closer look at Thomas More and his family. Painter Hans Holbein created this preliminary sketch of the More family prior to painting the family portrait.

painting was done and she was married by then, explaining the fact that her last name was different than her father's.

One person in from the left is Margaret Giggs. She is Thomas More's adopted daughter. She is putting on a pair of gloves.

The man seated next to Margaret Giggs is John More. He is Thomas More's father and he is welcomed and honored as a guest in his son's house. Throughout his life, Thomas More always honored his father.

Just behind John More is Anne Cresacre. She is 15 years old and is engaged to be married to John More, Thomas More's son. John stands holding a book. He is 19 years old.

Thomas More is at the center of the family portrait. He sits rather grandly, surrounded by his family. The portrait suggests his great success in life. Thomas More has used the knowledge and inspiration of his father, who sits at his right, to raise this large and healthy family.

As mentioned earlier, young John More stands to his father's left. John More has his head down and is studying a book. Like his father before him, young John More will always have good things to say about his father.

We continue moving to the right and find Henry Patenson. He is the only person who stares directly into the view of the portrait painter. Patenson was either blind or crazy at this time and he was the "fool" at the More household. Like a king or a queen at that time, Thomas More employed a fool to entertain himself and his family.

After Henry Patenson, moving down toward the front of the sketch, we find Cecily Heron, another of Thomas More's daughters. She is 20 years old. Moving over one more person, we find Margaret Roper, the eldest of Thomas More's daughters and the one he favored the most. She holds a book but looks rather directly toward the center of the gathering. For a woman of the time, she has a confident and self-assured expression.

Finally, moving once more to our right, we find Dame Alice More. She is Thomas More's second wife. He married her just a month after the death of his first wife, so that his children would have a mother to take care of them.

Looking at the portrait one more time, we see the importance of the clock. It hangs in the midsection of the painting, just above Thomas More. Many families of the time did not have clocks, so this was a valuable possession. Most likely, the portrait painter included it to show us the importance of time. Thomas More and his family are either reading, concentrating, or showing something to each other. They are not wasting time.

This family portrait reveals a rather remarkable scene. Here we see the members of an upper-class English family from the sixteenth century, presented to us as if we could walk directly into their living room—and into their lives.

There are also other ways of looking into the life of a family. One way is through letters that have been saved over the centuries. In 1517, ten years before Hans Holbein painted his portrait of the More family, Thomas More, who was then about 40 years old, sent a letter to his children. He began, "I hope that a letter to all of you may find my four children in good health and that your father's wishes may keep you so." [1] Everyone worried about health in the sixteenth century. People did not yet have access to the advanced medical treatments we enjoy today.

"In the meantime, while I make a long journey, drenched by a soaking rain, and while my mount, too frequently, is bogged down in the mud, I compose these verses for you."[2] Thomas More refers to writing "verses," but actually what followed were statements of prose, not poetry.

> It is not strange that I love you with my whole heart, for being a father is not a tie which can be ignored. Nature in her wisdom has attached the parent to the child and bound them spiritually together with a Herculean knot.[3]

Apparently, Thomas More was not afraid to write about his feelings of love for his children.

> But at this moment my love has increased so much that it seems to me I used not to love you at all. This feeling of mine is produced by your adult manners, adult despite your tender years; by your instincts, trained in noble principles which must be learned.[4]

Thomas More had been a schoolmaster from the very beginning—not in his public life, but in the private life of his household. He was one of the few Englishmen of the time to educate his daughters and his son. He was proud of their ability to read and write in Latin, and he encouraged them to

IOANNES HOLPENIVS BA: SILEENSIS
SVI IPSIVS EFFIGIATOR   Æ: XLV.

Painter Hans Holbein (shown here) provided a glimpse into the lives of the members of Thomas More's family.

become even better adults in the future. He ended with these words:

> Therefore, most dearly beloved children all, continue to endear yourselves to your father and, by those same accomplishments which make me think that I have not loved you before, make me think hereafter (if you can do it) that I do not love you now. [5]

These were the words of a devoted and loving father, but they are also the words of a schoolmaster. He wanted his children to continue along the path on which they were set. He wanted them to accomplish great things and to make him proud of them.

Test Your Knowledge

1   In what year was Thomas More made a saint of the Catholic Church?

    a. 1935

    b. 1359

    c. 1539

    d. 1953

2   When he painted the More family portrait, Hans Holbein was already a famous painter in what country?

    a. Austria

    b. Germany

    c. The Netherlands

    d. Switzerland

3   How old was Elizabeth Dauncy, one of Thomas More's daughters, when the family portrait was painted?

    a. 25

    b. 22

    c. 23

    d. 21

4   What one thing was everyone worried about in the sixteenth century?

    a. Marriage

    b. Wealth

    c. Health

    d. Children

5 Thomas More was one of very few Englishmen of his time to do what?

a. Marry multiple times

b. Educate his son and his daughters

c. Write letters to his children

d. All of the above

ANSWERS: 1. a; 2. b; 3. d; 4. c; 5. b

Father
and Son

homas More was born in London in February
1478. Historians are not sure of the exact day
of More's birth. What historians do know, however,
is that Thomas More was born into a dying era. The
Middle Ages were in their last years when More was
born. Although times and eras often cannot be dated

precisely, it is safe to say that by 1500, when Thomas More was 22, the Renaissance had replaced the Middle Ages.

The Middle Ages began after the fall of the Roman Empire, when Germanic tribes overran the empire in the fifth century. The long period known as the Middle Ages lasted for about 1,000 years. The Middle Ages were a time of deep and sincere religious beliefs. Christians throughout Europe viewed their time on Earth as a short term of penance, a time in which to do well in order to get to heaven. The Renaissance, which was in full swing during the life of Thomas More, celebrated life on Earth as well as good and valuable deeds. The great contradiction between the thinking of the Middle Ages and the ideas of the Renaissance would play out during Thomas More's life. He would be aware of both schools of thought and would respond to both, but he would never fully decide between them.

Thomas More was the son of John More and Agnes Graunger. We know very little about More's mother. She died when he was young and his father married three more times. So, during the course of his life, Thomas More had three different stepmothers. We do, however, know a good deal about his father.

John More was a man of inner-city London, a place where business is still conducted today. John More was also a hardworking, ambitious man, who had a passion for the law at an early age. He saw the transition from King Richard III, who was killed at the Battle of Bosworth Field, to King Henry VII, who won that battle. As a result of the Battle of Bosworth Field, King Henry VII started a new dynasty—the Tudor Dynasty—in honor of his family name.

John More rose in prestige steadily and surely throughout his life. He became a barrister, the English equivalent of a lawyer; a sergeant-at-arms; one of the officers of the city of London; and he was knighted later in life. He was a serious, careful man who performed his duties very well.

John More wanted a son to follow in his footsteps and he wanted that son to do even better, to bestow upon the family name even more acclaim. John More had high hopes for his son Thomas. Thomas More was probably named for Saint Thomas Beckett, who had been murdered at Canterbury Cathedral in 1170. Thomas was the most popular

Thomas More's father, John, was a man of inner-city London. He conducted business there and instilled in Thomas and his other children an appreciation for hard work. A view of London is shown here, with the old St. Paul's Cathedral and the old London Bridge in the background.

and most common name given to English boys at the time.

At the age of six, Thomas More started going to one of the best schools in London. Young Thomas got up early, before daylight, and walked with a candle in his hand to the school where he learned Latin, arithmetic, and rhetoric, or argument. He was a good student from the start.

At the age of 12, Thomas More received another task, his first real job in life. He became a page to the archbishop of Canterbury. The archbishop was the highest-ranking clergyman in all of England. He led prayers and devotions at Canterbury Cathedral, the place where Christianity first began in England. Just as important, the archbishop was often in London where the king called on him for advice and consultations. While the archbishop was in London, his needs were tended to by young pages, such as Thomas More.

The job of a page was not a hard one, but it meant staying alert at all times. Thomas More learned a great deal from his service to the archbishop. If John More had not already instilled in his son a lifelong respect for authority, surely Thomas More's job as a page was helping to do so. Throughout his life, Thomas More would be horrified whenever people rebelled against the authority of the Catholic Church, the king, or the nation.

Sometime around the age of 15, Thomas More went off to study at Oxford. It was not yet the great university that we know today, but it was already well respected. While there, Thomas More fell in love with learning. In fact, he never fell out of love with learning and it always remained the one great constant in his life. As we learned in Chapter 1, several members of the More family held a book when they were painted by Hans Holbein. This respect for learning and for expanding one's knowledge came to Thomas More from both his father and his time studying at Oxford.

Thomas More fell so deeply in love with learning that his father came to believe it was a dangerous pursuit. John More wanted his son to achieve, to make something of himself in the world, not just to learn new things for the sake of learning. John More knew there were already too many poor scholars, men who were easily led astray by their simple love of learning. He did not wish this to happen to his son. So, he pulled Thomas More out of Oxford and sent him to the legal schools of London. This, John More felt, was the best way to make a practical man out of his son.

Thomas More probably did not like the change much, but he was always a dutiful son. He went to school in London and soon did very well in his studies there. As the fifteenth century headed toward its final months, Thomas More was on his

London Then and Now

Thomas More would have trouble recognizing London in the twenty-first century. So much has changed since the time he walked the city streets. The Thames River still bends and curves in the same direction and the skies are still leaden and gray much of the time, with occasional spectacular breakthroughs of sun. Many other things have changed, however.

When Thomas More lived in London, it was home to fewer than 10,000 people. Today there are about 7 million people living in and around London, including the suburbs. When Thomas More went to Saint Paul's Cathedral, he saw a massive wooden church. It was later replaced by a massive stone building, finished around 1710. When Thomas More wanted to get away from the stone structures and busy streets of the city, he went to nearby grassy lawns, like those of way to becoming what his father had always wanted him to be—a successful Londoner.

Around this time, in the summer of 1499, Thomas More also befriended Desiderius Erasmus, who would remain a friend for life. A Dutchman by

Greenwich. Today, the people of London enjoy time in the many parks in the city itself.

There is, however, something timeless about London. Tourists come and go, and landmarks like Big Ben are built. New sites, such as the Millennium Wheel, attract attention, but then fade over time. Still the charm of the city lingers on.

London is still the center of the English-speaking world. Even though New York City has more money, and Washington D.C. has more political power, to see the nerve center of the English-speaking world, one needs to go to London. An eighteenth-century writer once said, "When a man is tired of London, he is tired of life; for there is in London all that life can afford."*

* London Quotes, "The Samuel Johnson Sound Bite Page," Available online at *http://www.samueljohnson.com/london.html.*

birth, Erasmus was about 12 years older than Thomas More. Erasmus had also lived a much harsher life than Thomas More. Erasmus's parents died when he was young and he entered a monastery—the only place that would take him. Bit by bit, however, Desiderius Erasmus climbed out of the poverty and loneliness that shaped his early life. In the summer of 1499, he came to England for the first time and stayed at the home of an English lord in the town of Greenwich, just outside of London.

When Thomas More and Erasmus met, they quickly became friends. They shared a love of Latin, Greek, and learning in general. They loved to write poems and often played jokes on each other. On one occasion, Thomas More came out well ahead in the exchange of practical jokes.

One summer day, Thomas More came to Greenwich and asked Erasmus to go with him on a long walk. Thomas More did not tell Erasmus where they were going. The two men meandered over the beautiful grassy lawns of Greenwich—which means "Green Town"—and then came to the gates of Eltham Palace, one of the residences of King Henry VII. He and Queen Elizabeth were not at the castle

Desiderius Erasmus and Thomas More shared a close friendship and a love of practical jokes. This panoramic image, entitled *View of Greenwich*, shows London in the distance.

that day, but their children, Prince Henry, Princess Margaret, and Princess Mary, were there. The fact that Thomas More and Erasmus were admitted to the royal household shows that the More family name was already known, both in London and among the members of the royal court. Years later, Erasmus recalled what happened.

Prince Henry was only eight years old, but he already showed an air of command. He and his sisters ate lunch at a high table while Thomas More and Erasmus ate their lunch at a lower table. During the meal, Prince Henry sent a page down to say that he expected a gift from Erasmus, who had brought nothing with him to give. Thomas More had already handed Prince Henry a poem or two, praising him and the royal family.

Erasmus was furious with Thomas More for not telling him where they were going and for leaving him without a gift to give. So Erasmus promised the page, and Prince Henry, that he would send lines of poetry the next day.

The joke had been on Erasmus this time. As Thomas More and Desiderius Erasmus walked away from the palace, Erasmus surely must have been angry with his friend. Desiderius Erasmus labored over his desk that night and sent many lines of poetry to the palace the next day. First, he wrote directly to the prince:

You ought to remember, most illustrious Duke Henry, that those persons who honor you with jewels or gold are giving you, first what is not their own, for such gifts belong to Fortune and are, moreover, perishable. . . . But someone who dedicates to you a poem which is the fruit of his own talent and sleepless toil offers, it seems to me, a present that is more distinguished.[6]

The lines having specifically to do with eight-year-old Prince Henry were as follows:

Now comes the boy Henry, who rejoices in having his father's name; guided to the sacred springs by the poet Skelton, he has trained himself in the arts of Athena from his tenderest years. How much of his father shines forth in his countenance![7]

John Skelton was an English poet who tutored Prince Henry in poetry, specifically the "arts of Athena." Erasmus's ode was well received by King Henry VII and the rest of the royal family. Little did they or anyone else know that the lives of Prince Henry, Erasmus, and Thomas More would be entwined for many years to come.

Test Your Knowledge

1 How long did the period known as the
Middle Ages last?
a. About 1,500 years
b. About 1,000 years
c. About 1,200 years
d. About 500 years

2 How many stepmothers did Thomas More
have during the course of his life?
a. Three
b. Four
c. Two
d. Five

3 John More saw the transition from King
Richard III to which king?
a. King Henry VIII
b. King Richard IV
c. King Henry VII
d. King Charles I

4 How old was Thomas More when he became
a page to the archbishop of Canterbury?
a. 15
b. 11
c. 14
d. 12

5 Thomas More and Desiderius Erasmus shared a love of

a. poetry.

b. animals.

c. winemaking.

d. nature.

ANSWERS: 1. b; 2. a; 3. c; 4. d; 5. a

A Rising Star

Throughout his life, Thomas More often said that he sought neither honor nor prestige. Still, every time he was offered a chance to move up in the world, he took it. Thomas More became an attorney in London around 1501 and he showed considerable talent right away. He was skilled at listening to the facts of a case and creating an argument out of those facts. His greatest admirers have often claimed that he used his skills to help the poor and underprivileged residents of London, but records show he was quite evenhanded. He neither looked down on the poor nor helped them to any great degree.

Thomas More's accomplishments were certainly due, in part, to the success of his father. John More had risen slowly but surely in life and he took great pleasure in his son's more rapid success. Having saved his son from the danger of a lifetime absorbed in the love of learning for its own sake, John More could now happily watch his son's progress as a lawyer.

Thomas More also began to think about marriage, but the subject was a source of conflict for him. Part of him also wanted to become a monk. He had read much about the beauty of monastic life and he felt he could dedicate himself to it. At the same time, however, he wanted a wife. We cannot be certain, but it is likely that his father, John More, played an important part in steering Thomas More toward marriage. John More was a very practical man. He surely believed that his son would be of little use if he never married and never had a family.

In those days, men who went into monasteries were referred to as being "dead to the world," meaning they had turned their back on family ties and their earlier life. In all likelihood, John More did not want to see this happen to his son, so he probably steered his son in the other direction.

Thomas More courted Jane Colt, the daughter of Sir John Colt of Essex. We do not know very much about the way they met or the way he courted her. This lack of information is not really all that unusual, however, as marriages in those days were often arranged by parents for their children. While this was not the case with Thomas More and Jane Colt, people generally put less emphasis on whether a man and woman were in love, and more importance on whether they would make a good match.

Of course, it is hard to predict which factors will create a good match. Some marriages look right on paper, but turn out to be less so in reality. We do know, however, that the marriage of Thomas More and Jane Colt started off very well.

When they married, in January 1505, John More was 26 years old and Jane Colt was about ten years younger. Soon after marriage, the couple moved into a new home in Bucklersbury, in the western end of London. Thomas More never again lived in his father's house. Marriage was enough to send him out into the world as an independent man.

Children followed soon enough. Margaret, the eldest, was born in 1506. Three other children soon followed, for a total of three daughters and one son. Thomas More was now a husband and a father. Naturally his life changed a great deal. More felt a responsibility to earn more money, in order to support his growing family. During these early years of married life, Thomas More began a rapid rise through higher levels of fame and fortune. He continued to practice law in London, but he also acquired other small tasks to earn extra income. Today, we would call Thomas More a member of the upper-middle class, but he probably thought he was barely making enough money. With his wife, children, and home to support, he needed all the income he could get.

Time seemed to move quickly for Thomas More. One thing standing in his way, however, was King Henry VII. In Chapter 1, we learned how Thomas More and Desiderius Erasmus met then-eight-year-old Prince Henry. He was not the heir to the throne at that time. His older brother, Arthur, was expected to succeed their father as king, but when Prince Arthur died soon after his marriage to the Spanish princess, Catherine of Aragon, young Prince Henry became the new heir to the throne.

It has always been hard to understand exactly why King Henry VII was so disliked by his people. He was a good, solid man who made the kingdom prosper. He brought the kingdom together after his victory at the Battle of Bosworth Field. He had a beautiful wife, Elizabeth of York, and four children (three of whom lived on after his death). Still, King Henry VII was heartily disliked. Perhaps people found him cold. Perhaps they thought he was too greedy with his money. Whatever the reasons, the people did not like their king.

Thomas More, like thousands of other English citizens, was not sad when King Henry VII died in April 1509, leaving the throne to his 18-year-old son, Prince Henry of Wales. Prince Henry quickly married Princess Catherine of Aragon, his brother's widow. Although there was a passage in the Bible prohibiting this practice, Prince Henry had received special dispensation from Pope Julius II. The couple

At the time of King Henry VII's death, Desiderius
Erasmus (shown here) was living the life of a poor
scholar in Italy. At the urging of a friend in Greenwich,
Erasmus returned to London to seek work under the
new king, Henry VIII.

were married in early June and crowned as king and queen in London on June 24, 1509.

Thomas More's diary does not tell us whether he attended the coronation ceremony, but he certainly liked having young Henry as the new king. Thomas More and his father, John More, had both disliked King Henry VII and they were thrilled by the change. Thomas More wrote in support of the new king:

> If ever there was a day, England, if ever there was a time for you to give thanks to those above, this is that happy day, one to be marked with a pure white stone and put in your calendar. . . . Now the people, freed, run before their king with bright faces. . . . The King is all that any mouth can say.[8]

At about the same time, Desiderius Erasmus, who was in Italy, learned that King Henry VII had died and had been replaced by King Henry VIII. Erasmus was still living the life of a poor scholar, making it day by day, worrying about where he would find his next meal. He was urged, in a letter from the English lord he knew from Greenwich, to

The Tudor Royal Family

The Tudor royal family began with King Henry VII, father to King Henry VIII. King Henry VII took the throne after he won the Battle of Bosworth Field in 1485. At that time, Thomas More was about seven years old. Thomas More remembered well the change in royal families. He later wrote a book, *Richard III*, condemning the man who lost the battle. Even so, Thomas More did not do very well during the reign of King Henry VII. He was much happier when King Henry VII died and was replaced by King Henry VIII.

Born in 1491, Henry VIII was 18 years old when he became king. He liked Thomas More from the very start. Sometimes the king invited Thomas More to join him on the deck or the roof of a royal palace, so they could look at the stars together. In his early years, King Henry VIII had a great love of learning.

King Henry VIII was a very active man. He hunted with a bow and arrow. He rode horseback in tournaments. He loved to laugh, sing, and dance. All of these things made him well loved by his subjects in the early part of his reign. Thomas More saw something else, though. He saw a man with great ambitions. He once wrote to a friend of his, "If my head would win him a castle in France, it should not fail to go."* Thomas More, as usual, saw something deeper than what was on the surface.

* Modern History Sourcebook, "William Roper: The Life of Sir Thomas More," Available online at *http://www.fordham.edu/halsall/mod/16Croper-more.html*.

come back to England where he hoped that King Henry VIII would find work for him.

Erasmus left Italy and headed for England. As he crossed the Alps, he wrote the first notes of what later became a very famous book, *In Praise of Folly.* When he first arrived in London, Erasmus went straight to the home of his friend Thomas More. When Erasmus arrived, he found that Thomas More had changed a great deal.

Test Your Knowledge

1   Thomas More became an attorney around
    what year?
    a. 1105
    b. 1501
    c. 1510
    d. 1115

2   How old was Thomas More when he got
    married?
    a. 21
    b. 24
    c. 26
    d. 22

3   How many children did Thomas More and
    his wife have?
    a. 4
    b. 3
    c. 5
    d. 2

4   Today we would call Thomas More a member
    of what class?
    a. Upper class
    b. Lower-middle class
    c. Middle class
    d. Upper-middle class

5 What did Erasmus do when he first arrived
in London?

a. He met the queen.

b. He got married.

c. He went to Thomas More's home.

d. He wrote a book.

ANSWERS: 1. b; 2. c; 3. a; 4. d; 5. c

Literary
Fame

I n 1509, Thomas More became the undersecretary to the treasurer of London. This was an important job, but not a very difficult one. The job brought Thomas More a second income and with it a measure of financial security. He had always made every effort to gain financial security. This instinct came naturally to him because of the influence of his father. Thomas More was working his way up in the world.

The accession of King Henry VIII to the throne was a definite plus for Thomas More. He now found it easier to go to court, to meet with the king, and to request certain jobs and assignments. Meanwhile, Jane Colt More was busy running the family household. She had married Thomas More when she was only 15 and she soon had four children to raise. Running a household and raising children were not easy tasks in the early 1500s, but she did both very well.

As Thomas More's influence and prestige increased, he became less concerned with taking primary responsibility for his family's welfare. He let his young wife handle most of the household matters until she died in 1511, after contracting a fever. Unfortunately, such deaths were very common in those days. Something called the "sweating sickness" passed through England every few years. It was not as deadly as the bubonic plague, but all Englishmen and women considered their health to be at risk much of the time.

Jane Colt was buried in the More family plot and, less than one month later, Thomas More married again. His second wife, Alice Middleton, was the widow of a London merchant and she had a daughter, also named Alice. Thomas More's new wife was a few years older than he was and it was unlikely she would ever give birth to more children. Thomas More saw her as an excellent addition to the family, however. He wanted a manager for the household and a mother for his four young children.

Many people have commented on the haste of Thomas More's second marriage, wondering why he married so soon, just one month after the death of Jane Colt More. To some, the haste seemed positively indecent. All we really know for sure is that Thomas More generally acted with certainty and promptness. The clock on the wall of the family portrait, discussed in Chapter 1, shows that Thomas More always viewed time as something of great importance.

At about the same time that he married Alice Middleton, Thomas More also played host to Desiderius Erasmus. When Erasmus came to London in the summer of 1511, he found that Thomas More had changed a great deal. The two men had first met in the summer of 1499, when they were both scholars and practical jokers. They met again in the summer of 1505, when Thomas More was a newly married man. Now, Thomas More was a family man, married for the second time. He was also accustomed to making money through the practice of law.

Erasmus was disappointed by the changes in his old friend, but he felt even worse about Thomas More's new wife. Alice Middleton More was a serious, severe household manager. She did not approve of Desiderius Erasmus and other "freeloading" guests whom her husband invited into their home. Not long after he arrived at the More home, Desiderius Erasmus began to feel pressure to leave, but he would not go before he completed his literary masterpiece, *In Praise of Folly*. Thomas More's last name was used as part of the title. In Latin, *More* meant something close to folly. Therefore the title could also be interpreted to mean something similar to *In Praise of More.*

The book became a bestseller in the sixteenth century. In the book, folly appears in the guise of a fool, dressed as a woman. She lectures to a crowd, telling them that folly, or foolishness, is much more important than they think. What, she

Desiderius Erasmus came to visit Thomas More shortly after More married Alice Middleton. During this time, Erasmus completed his literary masterpiece, *In Praise of Folly*. The frontispiece of the first French edition of the book, published in 1520, is shown here.

asks, would ever happen in the world if folly were not around?

No one would ever start a business and no one would ever start a career if they knew how much labor was involved. Positively no one would ever marry or have children if they knew how hard those things would be. For all of these reasons, folly is essential, vital for the survival of the human race.

Some people did not like *In Praise of Folly*. Erasmus attacked the Catholic Church and many members of the clergy in his book. He made them sound like hypocritical fools, always repeating the prayers of saints from the distant past. In a way, *In Praise of Folly* was a call for a more rational, more modern type of religion.

Thomas More liked the book. He and Erasmus continued to be friends even after Erasmus left the Mores' home. Erasmus really could not stay there because of Alice More, whom everyone now called Dame More. She was probably right, however, in seeing Erasmus and others among her husband's friends as lazy freeloaders.

Regardless of his wife's views, Thomas More was quite inspired by Desiderius Erasmus. The two men had always thought along similar lines. They both liked the new humanism movement, which showed an appreciation of the good deeds performed by humans. Even though he was busy being a lawyer and the undersecretary for the London treasury, and performing other tasks, Thomas More began to compose what would become his own literary masterpiece.

Utopia was published in 1516, and the world has never been quite the same since. The word *utopia* means "nowhere" or "no place" in Latin. This "no place" is what Thomas More describes in his book. *Utopia* contains two parts. In the first part, Thomas More meets a tired, red-faced sailor, who has traveled around vast parts of the world. This sailor tells him about an island called Utopia, ruled by a man called Utopus.

In the second part of the book, More provides a detailed description of the people and places of Utopia. We learn that the people of Utopia hold all property in common. In our modern world, we call this system of government Communism. Under Communism, no one really owns anything. People have the right to use certain things, as long as other people in the community agree, but everything can be taken away if the people in the community agree that this is the right thing to do.

We live in a very different world. Our world view is shaped by the idea of private property ownership. What people earn through work or good luck is theirs to keep. No one can take it away. The people of England in the sixteenth century also believed in

Books in the Sixteenth Century

The bestselling book of all time is the Bible. More copies of the Bible have been printed, bought, and sold than any other book in history. The art of book printing started around 1450, in the Rhineland region of Germany. Printers there found out how to use interchangeable pieces of metal, shaped as letters, and made printed sheets by using a machine called the printing press. There was no electricity involved. Printers used physical strength to press the sheets of paper onto the inked metal letters.

When Thomas More came into the world in 1478, the printing press was less than 30 years old, but it was already making its mark. This progress is one of the reasons we say that Thomas More was born into a dying age. The ways of the Middle Ages, with people private property, so the ideas in *Utopia* came as a shock to them.

Thomas More also discusses social customs, such as marriage. In *Utopia*, he describes how Utopian men and women examine each other before marriage. A man and a woman have to be sure they are getting a healthy person for a husband or

being informed by handmade copies of manuscripts, were being replaced by the ways of the Renaissance, with people being informed by printed books.

Desiderius Erasmus and Thomas More were two of the first bestselling authors of their time. *In Praise of Folly* and *Utopia* were among the biggest sellers of the entire sixteenth century and they continue to be read today. Though they did not intend it, Erasmus and Thomas More helped to advance the stature of the writer as an artist. Their books came out around the same time that the artist Michelangelo finished painting the ceiling of the Sistine Chapel in Rome. Efforts like those made by Erasmus, Thomas More, and Michelangelo increased the status of the artist in the new world of the Renaissance.

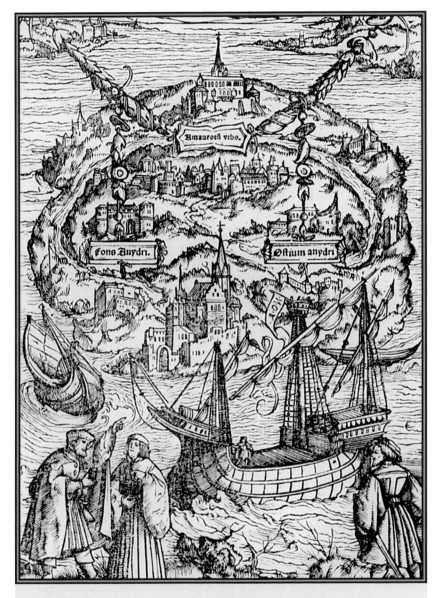

Thomas More's literary masterpiece, *Utopia,* was published in 1516. In one part of the book, More describes the people and places of the fictional island of Utopia. A map of the island is shown here.

wife, so they are allowed, with a chaperone, to take off each other's clothes. This, too, was shocking to many readers.

Thomas More also describes how Utopians wage war. They love peace, he says, but when they go to war they do so with a vengeance. They often bring captured people home and make them slaves. In addition, Thomas More brings up the subject of land enclosures. In his time, wealthy men in England were buying up all of the available land. They fenced off the land they bought, thereby enclosing it and preventing further use by other people's horses and cattle. Thomas More was clearly against the enclosure of land. He shows, in *Utopia*, how the people of that island prevented this from happening on their land.

We could say a lot more about *Utopia*. It is not a very long book, but it is so full of ideas, thoughts, and morals, all cleverly disguised, that one can spend a lifetime reading and rereading it. *Utopia* was one of the greatest books of the sixteenth century and it remains one of the great classics of today. Thomas More had fulfilled many of his desires. He had become a husband, a father, a property owner, and a published author in London. He also had many friends, some of them in high places. His ideas would continue to be discussed and debated for centuries after he was gone.

Test Your Knowledge

1   In what year did Thomas More become
the undersecretary to the treasurer of
London?

a. 1590

b. 1509

c. 1500

d. 1550

2   How old was Jane Colt when she married
Thomas More?

a. 15

b. 17

c. 18

d. 20

3   How did Thomas More's first wife die?

a. After falling from a horse

b. During childbirth

c. After contracting a fever

d. As a result of a rare disease

4   What does the word *utopia* mean in Latin?

a. "Everlasting love"

b. "No where" or "no place"

c. "Unending joy"

d. "Forever"

5 Our world view is shaped by the idea of

    a. private property.

    b. wealth.

    c. materialism.

    d. all of the above.

ANSWERS: 1. a; 2. b; 3. c; 4. b; 5. a

The King's Servant

T homas More had much to be pleased with in his life. At the same time, however, the demands on his time increased with his growing literary fame. In fact, King Henry VIII made Thomas More one of his most important servants. A king such as Henry VIII had many servants in his palace. Some of them washed dishes. Others prepared meals or made beds. Still others, such as the king's fool, were there purely for the king's amusement.

A servant such as Thomas More, however, served an entirely different purpose. He was a man of substance, someone whose advice the king might seek. He was someone who was "on call" whenever the king needed him. A servant such as Thomas More was a free man, but he could find himself in serious trouble if he displeased the king. Such servants were said to serve "at the pleasure of the king." Thomas More was no ordinary servant. He was a man of some importance in the royal court.

At first, King Henry VIII liked having Thomas More around. More knew a great deal about literature, science, and world events. The king and his servant often watched the stars together from the roof of one of the royal palaces. As time went on, King Henry VIII started to depend on Thomas More for advice. Thomas More had spent a great deal of time practicing the law. So, his legal knowledge was very useful to King Henry. As more time passed, King Henry VIII also started giving diplomatic assignments to Thomas More.

Thomas More's rise in importance was paralleled by that of Thomas Wolsey. A little older than Thomas More, Thomas Wolsey was the son of a butcher. This fact was enough to encourage snickers behind his back when he became the king's chief minister, or servant. Thomas Wolsey was also a very ambitious man who made many enemies during his rise to the top. Perhaps Thomas More's claim that he had never sought power or distinction was meant to show that he was not at all like Thomas Wolsey. Regardless, the two men rose in the king's ranks together.

By the end of 1515, Thomas Wolsey was King Henry VIII's prime minister. Thomas More had become a member of the king's council. All was not fun and games in the royal court, however. There was a conflict forming between England and France. King Henry VIII nursed a special grudge against neighboring France. So, King Henry sent Thomas More on a special diplomatic trip to the town of Calais, on the French side of the English Channel.

Thomas More and his fellow diplomats wrote to the king's council:

Thomas More's rise in importance among the members of King Henry VIII's court was matched by that of Thomas Wolsey. Wolsey (shown here) became King Henry VIII's prime minister. Thomas More became a member of the king's council.

And as your good lordships well know, that we had so short warning for this journey, that our time was very little and scarce to prepare ourselves and our company forward. . . . Wherefore we beseech your good lordships, that as your wisdoms perceive, that we be like here to abide, so it would like you to order that we may have money sent us.[9]

Thomas More had a large family to support and being away so often on some of these diplomatic assignments created financial hardships for his family. He could not, however, refuse the requests of the king, especially a king like Henry VIII. The king had a reputation for turning against people who displeased him. So, Thomas More continued to travel on diplomatic assignments, as needed.

Between 1516 and 1520, Thomas More rose continually in the king's service. The only reason he did not attract more attention and more envy was because Thomas Wolsey had become far more prestigious. Wolsey had been the king's almoner—in charge of distributing alms to the poor—when Henry VIII came to the throne. Soon Wolsey was named as the cardinal of York and the chief minister to the king, along with many other titles. To show off his greatness, Cardinal Wolsey had a vast new palace built upriver from London on the Thames. This became Hampton Court Palace.

Some historians think that King Henry VIII gave up control over most of the government, leaving Cardinal Wolsey to basically run the kingdom for about ten years. This was probably not true. Like all kings and queens, King Henry VIII had to find capable and able servants to handle most

The Court of King Henry VIII

The court of King Henry VIII was, beyond any doubt, the most dazzling and expensive court England had ever seen. When he came to the throne at age 18, King Henry decided to spend as much money as was necessary to make him and his court seem glorious and powerful. While his father, King Henry VII, had saved and scrimped to keep money in the royal treasury, King Henry VIII spent with no regard for the consequences.

The court traveled at different times to Eltham Palace in Greenwich, to Windsor Castle west of London, and later to Hampton Court Palace, upstream from London on the Thames River. All of the palaces were decorated in the finest style. Hampton Court Palace was especially beautiful. A huge clock was visible to everyone who entered. The famous astronomical clock told the time in England and indicated when the tides rose and fell at Greenwich.

of the details of government, to avoid being overwhelmed. He still maintained control over his kingdom, however.

While Cardinal Wolsey became the second-most-powerful man in England, Thomas More carefully added to his own list of titles and perks—known in

On a lighter note, we might say that King Henry's court was very good for the development of music and dance. The king played the lute. Queen Catherine played the harp and, between them, they inspired many nobles to become musicians. The king was, for a long time, the best dancer at his own court, and Tudor music remains popular even today. The quickstep dance tunes of the sixteenth century have a timeless quality to them.

Most of the palaces from King Henry VIII's time are still in royal hands today. This is not true of the homes of many other great nobles. Quite a few families had to sell their estates over the centuries. Those that still have their homes often have to open parts of them to tourists, in order to pay for the upkeep.

those days as perquisites. More never became truly rich, but he was able to move his family from Bucklersbury, which had been nice enough, to Chelsea, just outside of London. It was there that Hans Holbein completed his famous painting of the More family.

Thomas More had a chance to see Desiderius Erasmus again in the spring of 1520. In fact, Thomas More had the chance to see many important people from England and France when the great festival known as the Field of Cloth of Gold was held just outside of Calais, on the French side of the English Channel.

For some time, the kings of England and France had wanted to get together for a great conference. The members of the royal courts of both nations were also eager to come together. There would be opportunities for horsemanship, swordplay, and other challenges. All of Cardinal Thomas Wolsey's abilities were needed to organize this great event.

King Henry VIII brought some 6,000 men and women with him to the Field of the Cloth of Gold. King Francis I of France brought an equal number of people. One has only to consider how much beef

The great festival known as the Field of the Cloth of Gold was held just outside of Calais, on the French side of the English Channel. King Henry VIII rides in (at left) to meet King Francis I.

the nobles of that time ate, and how much ale they drank, to take in the staggering amount of food and beverages consumed by some 12,000 leading citizens of England and France.

For this event, Thomas More was a rather unimportant member of the king's entourage. As much as King Henry liked Thomas More, and as much as the king valued More's advice, Thomas More was neither a horseman nor a swordsman. This, therefore, was not the time to show off his skills. While King Henry and King Francis had a great time, holding tournaments in which English and French nobles rode against each other, Thomas More enjoyed a quieter time. He met with his old friend Desiderius Erasmus and with Guilluame Buade, a French scholar he had never met before.

When the Field of the Cloth of Gold broke up after two weeks, Erasmus rode back to his home in Belgium. Thomas More went back to England by ship. Nothing very important was achieved at the conference, which was unfortunate because the kings of both England and France were about to face a formidable new challenge. It was called Lutheranism and it would eventually change into Protestantism, and alter the face of religion. The religious unity of the Middle Ages was about to be shattered.

Test Your Knowledge

1 King Henry VIII depended on Thomas
   More for

   a. performing religious ceremonies.

   b. financial support.

   c. advice.

   d. reciting poetry.

2 Thomas Wolsey was the son of

   a. a merchant.

   b. a butcher.

   c. a banker.

   d. a farmer.

3 By the end of 1515, there was a conflict
   between England and

   a. France.

   b. Spain.

   c. Germany.

   d. Italy.

4 Cardinal Wolsey became

   a. the mayor of London.

   b. a banker.

   c. the pope.

   d. the second-most-powerful man
      in England.

5   How many men and women did King Henry VIII bring with him to the Field of the Cloth of Gold?

a. 5,000

b. 6,000

c. 3,000

d. 4,500

ANSWERS: 1. c; 2. b; 3. a; 4. d; 5. b

Martin Luther's Challenge

Thomas More and Martin Luther, the founder of Lutheranism, never met, which was probably for the best. They hated each other quite heartily, even from a distance. Martin Luther was a German monk, born about five years after Thomas More. On the surface, Martin Luther and Thomas More seemed to come from rather similar circumstances.

Like Thomas More, Martin Luther had an ambitious father. Like Thomas More, Martin Luther was also pressured by his father to become an important lawyer, a man of business. (Later in life, however, More would mock the tireless pursuit of "busyness.") Unlike Thomas More, Martin Luther broke away from his father and from his family's desires, when he became a monk around 1505, and the differences between the two men did not end there.

In the summer of 1517, Martin Luther became upset by the number of indulgences that were being sold in his part of Germany. An indulgence, an official piece of paper issued by the Roman Catholic Church, was intended to reduce the time that a person's dead relatives would spend in purgatory. Indulgences were not intended to help the person who bought them. This did not, however, prevent ambitious salespeople from selling many indulgences to people who had the mistaken idea that they could lessen their own time in purgatory.

In the summer of 1517, Martin Luther became upset by the number of indulgences that were being sold in his part of Germany by the Roman Catholic Church. In response, he posted the 95 Theses on the door of the church in Wittenberg, Germany, as dramatized in this picture.

Martin Luther became so upset with this practice that he wrote a long list of statements and nailed them on the door of the church in Wittenberg, Germany. Known as the 95 Theses, Luther's statements challenged concerned citizens to come and debate the matter of indulgences in person.

If the Roman Catholic Church had made any effort at reform, Martin Luther probably would have been easily appeased. After all, Luther did not hate the church. Much like Thomas More, some 600 miles away, Martin Luther also loved the church. Because the pope and other church leaders refused to create any reforms, however, Luther continued his statements. King Henry VIII and Thomas More were both upset by the statements of Martin Luther.

In the winter of 1521, King Henry VIII wrote a book in Latin against Martin Luther's views. The king was a fine writer in Latin and he was quite intelligent. Still, it is likely he had help from Thomas More and some other members of the royal council to write his book. Without help, the writing of the book probably would have taken much longer. In the summer of 1521, King Henry VIII sent a copy of the new book to Pope Leo X in Rome. The pope responded by declaring that King Henry VIII and all of his heirs should receive the permanent title of "Defender of the Faith." All English kings and queens, including those of today, have used this as one of their official titles.

King Henry's book was called *Defense of the Seven Sacraments.* In it, King Henry VIII defended the traditional seven sacraments of the Roman Catholic faith. In contrast, Martin Luther's statements had declared that only two of the sacraments were true.

Thomas More may have stood by King Henry's side and helped him compose some of the work. Scholars believe, however, that Thomas More urged King Henry to tone down his defense of Pope Leo X and the Roman Catholic Church. If King Henry defended Pope Leo too strongly, the king would not be able to disagree with the pope on any matters at all. King Henry seems to have taken Thomas More's advice.

Defense of the Seven Sacraments was a bold blow in the war of words between the king and Martin Luther. Not surprisingly, Martin Luther struck back. His answer was another book entitled *Against Henry, King of the English.* Martin Luther had a fierce temper and sometimes a foul mouth, as well. He attacked King Henry VIII in language that was sometimes obscene. There had to be an answer to his profanity, and that task fell to Sir Thomas More, who had recently been knighted by King Henry VIII.

Thomas More loved to write elegant prose. He loved words for their own sake. Few men of the

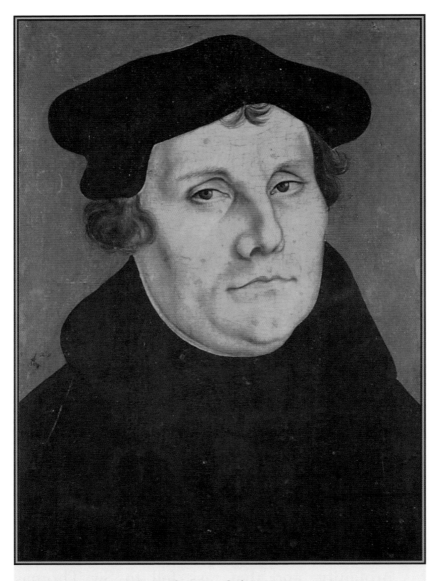

King Henry VIII's *Defense of the Seven Sacraments* defended the traditional seven sacraments of the Roman Catholic faith. Martin Luther (shown here) answered with another book entitled *Against Henry, King of the English.*

time could compete with him—in English or in Latin. Unfortunately, when Thomas More wrote *Response to Luther*, in 1522, he took his task so personally that his words sunk to Luther's crude level. Many of Thomas More's arguments were well phrased, but he too used profanity in his war of words against Martin Luther.

At about the same time, Thomas More experienced yet another boost to his career. In the summer of 1523, King Henry VIII wanted and needed the House of Lords and the House of Commons to pass a larger-than-usual tax. In an effort to get the tax passed, King Henry VIII and Cardinal Thomas Wolsey appointed Thomas More as the speaker of the House of Commons.

More was not a natural politician. He did love to speak, however, and the position of speaker gave him the perfect opportunity to do so. More did his best for the king and the cardinal, but the tax amount agreed to by the House of Commons was less than what was desired. Even so, Cardinal Wolsey wrote to King Henry to say that Thomas More had done his very best. He was a faithful and loyal servant to the crown.

Thomas More and Martin Luther

Despite similarities in their early lives, the two men could hardly have been more different. One believed firmly in the Roman Catholic Church. The other wanted to reform that church. When reform was not possible, he started a new church. Thomas More's father had been able to talk him out of becoming a monk. Martin Luther's father tried as well, but he failed. Martin Luther became a monk in 1505.

Once the battle began between those who followed Martin Luther, known as the Lutherans, and Roman Catholics who followed the pope, Martin Luther and Thomas More became bitter enemies. They never met, but they traded blows in their written works.

Thomas More started out as a lawyer and an author, but he became Lord Chancellor to King Henry VIII in 1529, allowing him to hunt down and prosecute the followers of Martin Luther in England. Thomas More clearly liked this part of his work. Like many people of his time, he believed there should be no mercy for heretics. Anyone who willfully went against the edicts of the Roman Catholic Church should be severely punished.

By the mid-1520s, Thomas More had many reasons to be satisfied. He was a successful lawyer, an able servant of the crown, and he was providing for his large and growing family. Two of his daughters were married on the same day in 1525 and Thomas More looked forward to seeing his future grandchildren.

Test Your Knowledge

1 Like Thomas More, Martin Luther
a. started a new religion.
b. had an ambitious father.
c. became a monk.
d. had four children.

2 Martin Luther's 95 Theses challenged people to
a. go to church more often.
b. live better lives.
c. debate the matter of indulgences.
d. become better Christians.

3 Martin Luther's statements had declared that only how many of the sacraments were true?
a. Five
b. Three
c. Four
d. Two

4 In an effort to get a tax passed, King Henry VIII and Cardinal Thomas Wolsey appointed Thomas More as
a. speaker of the House of Commons.
b. tax assessor.
c. court accountant.
d. ambassador to France.

5 Two of Thomas More's daughters were married on the same day in what year?

a. 1545

b. 1525

c. 1555

d. 1515

King Henry's Great Matter

During 1527, something began to develop in King Henry VIII's court. Lawyers, nobles, and even common people began calling this new development the king's Great Matter. By 1527, King Henry VIII had been married for 18 years. His wife, Queen Catherine of Aragon, was a Spanish princess. She had first married Henry's older brother, Prince Arthur, but, when the prince died within six months of their wedding, Catherine and Henry were married in 1509 and crowned as king and queen of England.

During the course of their 18-year marriage, Queen Catherine had not given birth to a son. At the time, the lack of a male heir presented a great problem. King Henry VIII wanted to leave the throne, and the kingdom, to a son. He believed that only under the leadership of a son would the kingdom be secure.

By 1527, King Henry had grown tired of Queen Catherine's inability to produce a male heir. He had found a new love in his life. She was Anne Boleyn, daughter of Sir Thomas Boleyn, one of King Henry's diplomats. She had spent her first ten years at home in England, before spending several years at royal courts in France and Holland. She was an enchanting young woman with beautiful dark hair. She knew all about the fashions from Holland and France, and she brought them to the court of King Henry VIII. By 1527, the king had fallen deeply in love with Anne Boleyn.

Catherine of Aragon, the first wife of King Henry VIII, is shown here. When, after 18 years of marriage, Queen Catherine was unable to produce a male heir to the throne, King Henry VIII found a new love.

Thomas More was still a good friend and a counselor to King Henry VIII. Years later, Thomas More remembered that King Henry first brought up the subject of divorce in 1527. King Henry wanted to divorce Queen Catherine so that he could marry Anne Boleyn, but he needed to figure out how this could be done. Thomas More was not in favor of this change. He liked Queen Catherine and knew that the people of London were also very fond of her. For that reason alone, he advised the king not to seek a divorce.

Other members of the royal court reacted differently. Cardinal Thomas Wolsey had made his name, his fame, and his living by always providing whatever the king wanted. Cardinal Wolsey now promised to find a way for the king to divorce the queen.

The king's Great Matter became even more complicated during that spring and summer. In May 1527, the unpaid soldiers of Emperor Charles V attacked the city of Rome. The emperor had not ordered the soldiers to go to war, but his soldiers went ahead, attacking and capturing the city. Pope Clement VII was forced to flee. He found refuge in Castle San Angelo, on the banks of the Tiber River—the only secure place in Rome, from which he could not venture out. From that day on, Pope Clement VII became a virtual prisoner of the unpaid soldiers of Emperor Charles V.

Queen Catherine of England was the aunt of Emperor Charles V, and he did not wish to see his aunt humiliated or disgraced. Only Pope Clement

Queen Catherine of England

Born in 1485, Catherine of Aragon was a Spanish princess. Her mother was Queen Isabella, the Spanish queen who sent Christopher Columbus to the New World. Princess Catherine came to England in 1502 and married Prince Arthur, the heir to the English throne. When he died just six months later, she became a widow as a young woman.

For years, she withered away at the court of King Henry VII. Then he died and the new king, Henry VIII, made her his bride. To do so, King Henry had to obtain a special dispensation from Pope Julius II. Eighteen years passed. In that time, Queen Catherine had one child, Princess Mary. There were no sons, no heirs to King Henry's throne.

VII could issue a dispensation, which would allow King Henry to divorce his wife. Remember, Pope Julius II had issued a dispensation so that King Henry could marry Catherine in the first place. All of this was very complicated, but it boiled down to this fact—King Henry wanted a divorce and Pope Clement VII would not grant him one.

King Henry was madly in love with Anne Boleyn and, in 1533, he married her in secret. Months later, he granted himself a divorce. He was able to do this because he had made himself the leader of the Church of England. Poor Queen Catherine was separated from her beloved daughter, Princess Mary. Catherine was sent to a damp old castle in England and kept away from the court. She died in 1536.

King Henry VIII had a total of six wives. His marriage to Catherine lasted for 18 years. The other wives were not so lucky. As one ballad put it, out of the six, "two divorced, two beheaded, one died, and one survived."[*]

[*] Nationmaster.com Encyclopedia, "Henry VIII of England," Available online at *http://www.nationmaster.com/encyclopedia/Henry_VIII_of_England*.

During 1527 and 1528, King Henry VIII kept trying to find a way to get a divorce. His counselors and lawyers assured him that the only way to end his marriage was to have a public hearing with a representative from the pope present. In June 1529, King Henry VIII summoned a court at Blackfriars, with Cardinal Campeggio from Rome present. Historians do not know much about Thomas More's advice at the time. They are not sure if he persisted in telling King Henry VIII that the divorce was a bad idea. They do know, however, that the court at Blackfriars helped to bring about the downfall of Cardinal Thomas Wolsey.

Part of the reason for Cardinal Wolsey's decline was the great skill with which Queen Catherine conducted herself at the court hearing. She fell to her knees in front of King Henry and begged him to tell her how she had offended him. King Henry looked away, deeply embarrassed. Everyone knew Queen Catherine had been a model wife in all ways but one. She had one daughter, Princess Mary, but she had not provided the king with any sons.

Queen Catherine almost won the day. If King Henry had not been deeply, madly in love with

The public hearing about King Henry's divorce from Catherine of Aragon is shown here. Queen Catherine's inability to produce a son, and King Henry VIII's deep love for Ann Boleyn, ensured that the trial would not go well for Queen Catherine.

Anne Boleyn, he might have listened to his advisors and given up on the whole Great Matter. Unfortunately for Queen Catherine, he was crazy about Anne Boleyn and he insisted on marrying her.

Cardinal Campeggio was the representative for Pope Clement VII. The pope and Cardinal Campeggio had two reasons for being against the divorce. First, Cardinal Clement was practically a prisoner of the troops of Emperor Charles, Queen Catherine's nephew. Second, Pope Clement VII did not wish to reverse a decision that Pope Julius had made in the past. To do so would confirm many of the accusations made by Martin Luther against the Roman Catholic Church. For both of these reasons, the papacy opposed King Henry's divorce. Cardinal Campeggio left England with the Great Matter still unresolved.

Meanwhile, Cardinal Wolsey, who had promised King Henry he would solve the Great Matter, now feared for his estates and his life. Everyone knew that King Henry had a horrible temper when things did not go his way. Early in September, King Henry had his last visit with Cardinal Wolsey. King Henry assured the cardinal that he still favored him and that all would be well, but there were two other men conspiring against Cardinal Wolsey.

The Duke of Suffolk and the Duke of Norfolk had always disliked Cardinal Wolsey. The two dukes were men of prestigious families with valuable lands and estates. They thought they should be the ones to advise the king. Instead, Thomas Wolsey, the son of a butcher, had risen to take their place as the king's primary advisor.

The Duke of Norfolk and the Duke of Suffolk joined together to persuade King Henry that Cardinal Wolsey was a bad man who had turned against the king. In October 1529, Cardinal Wolsey was told he was no longer Lord Chancellor of England. The two dukes required him to return the gilded neck chain that was the symbol of his office. Thomas Wolsey sent letters to King Henry, begging the king to see him, but the letters were returned. Thomas Wolsey, who had enjoyed the king's favor for so long, was now experiencing the pain of losing that favor.

Test Your Knowledge

1 By 1527, King Henry VIII had been married to Catherine of Aragon for how many years?

    a. 20

    b. 17

    c. 15

    d. 18

2 The king's Great Matter involved

    a. divorce.

    b. money.

    c. religion.

    d. politics.

3 King Henry had grown tired of

    a. Queen Catherine's flirting with other men.

    b. Queen Catherine's inability to produce a male heir.

    c. Queen Catherine's lavish spending habits.

    d. Queen Catherine's constant need for attention.

4 In May 1527, the unpaid soldiers of Emperor Charles V attacked the city of

    a. London.

    b. Florence.

    c. Rome.

    d. Oxford.

5 What was Queen Catherine's relationship to Emperor Charles V?

a. She was his aunt.

b. She was his sister.

c. She was his mother.

d. She was his daughter.

ANSWERS: 1. d; 2. a; 3. b; 4. c; 5. a

Thomas More, Lord Chancellor

The honor of advising King Henry and the title of Lord Chancellor of England now belonged to Thomas More, who became Lord Chancellor in December 1529. Throughout his life, Thomas More liked to say that he had never sought high office, but that the offices had simply come to him. This was not always true. He had liked being the undersherriff for London and being a member of King Henry VIII's council, but Thomas More probably did not wish to become Lord Chancellor. This position was full of responsibility and danger. Still, no one could turn down an appointment from King Henry VIII. That would be even more dangerous than accepting the post. So, Thomas More took the new position.

Around this time, in the autumn of 1529, there was a large fire at Chelsea, where Thomas More lived. All of his barns and cornfields were destroyed. At the time of the fire, Thomas More was at court, in the service of the king. He could not return to Chelsea because he was busy attending to the king's business. After learning of the fire, Thomas More wrote a letter to his wife, one of the few people who had survived:

Mistress Alice, in my most heart way I recommend me to you.

And whereas I am informed by my son Heron of the loss of our barns and our neighbors also with all the corn that was therein, albeit (saving God's pleasure) it were greater pity of so much good corn lost, yet sayeth it hath liked him to send us such a chance, we must and are bounden not only to be content but also to be glad of his visitation.

He sent us all that we have lost and sayeth he has by such a chance taken away that again his pleasure be fulfilled; let us never grudge thereat but take in good worth and heartily thank him as well for adversity as for prosperity.[10]

Thomas More went on to ask his wife to inquire about how much the neighbors had lost. He concluded, "And thus as heartily fare you well with all our children as you can wish, at Woodstock the third day of September, by the hand of your loving husband, Thomas More, Knight."[11]

This letter provides the only real sense of the nature of the relationship between Thomas More and his wife. They seem to have had a rather businesslike relationship, with her providing household management and him being the connection to the outside world.

The letter also indicated that Thomas More remained very much a man of faith. Even though he was Lord Chancellor, the second-most-important man in the land, he still recommended to his wife that they thank God for adversity as well as for prosperity.

Serving as the king's most important advisor was an entirely different matter, however. At first, the job was not too burdensome. The Duke of Norfolk and the Duke of Suffolk were only too glad to be the chief advisors to King Henry VIII. They whispered in the king's ear on all sorts of matters, while Thomas More applied himself to matters of justice in the kingdom. After all, law had always been one of Thomas More's great interests. He had practiced law for many years and now he could make some improvements in the legal system. Unfortunately, his anger against the Lutherans, or Protestants, was now intense.

Thomas More had always been a faithful follower of the teachings of the Roman Catholic Church. Now he had the power to make other people follow the rules of the church. Heretics, those who did not follow the church, would be brought to justice. Thomas More never had anyone tortured in front of him, but he did send men to the torture chamber, knowing what would happen to them. He

Sir Thomas More (shown here) was a faithful follower of the teachings of the Roman Catholic Church. As the king's most important advisor, More had the power to make sure other people followed the teachings of the church.

wanted to ensure that the Roman Catholic faith remained the law of the land.

Just ten years earlier, King Henry VIII and Thomas More had seen matters of religion in the same way. Both of them had loved and defended the Catholic Church. King Henry had even received the title of "Defender of the Faith." Unfortunately, however, Cardinal Wolsey had not been able to solve the king's Great Matter, so it dragged on. The Duke of Norfolk and the Duke of Suffolk were also unable to solve it. Chancellor Thomas More did not wish to solve it. He wanted the king to forget about it, for the good of the kingdom. Thomas Cromwell, master secretary to King Henry VIII, stepped forward.

Thomas Cromwell and Thomas More had known each other for years. Both of them had served the king while Cardinal Wolsey was Lord Chancellor. Thomas Cromwell was now the chief secretary to King Henry VIII, and Cromwell proposed a radical solution to the king's Great Matter. Because the Roman Catholic pope would not grant a divorce, King Henry could break away from Rome and create an English Catholic Church.

Thomas Cromwell (shown here) was chief secretary to King Henry VIII. Cromwell proposed a radical solution to the king's Great Matter. Because the Roman Catholic pope would not grant a divorce, Cromwell advised King Henry to break away from Rome and create an English Catholic Church.

This would mean a break with more than 1,000 years of tradition. England had been Roman Catholic since the early Middle Ages.

Thomas Cromwell told King Henry that he did not need to change any part of the Catholic Church. The bishops, Mass, and the sacraments could all remain, with King Henry himself as the new pope, or supreme head of the church.

King Henry was not eager to break from Roman Catholic tradition. He had argued for the power of the pope in his book against Martin Luther. He was, however, still madly in love with Anne Boleyn. He desperately needed a divorce. Because Thomas Cromwell was the only person who proposed a real solution, King Henry put the matter in Cromwell's hands.

Thomas Cromwell should have been more cautious. He should have remembered what had happened to Cardinal Wolsey. Instead, Thomas Cromwell pushed the Great Matter forward. King Henry announced that the bishops of England would need to swear allegiance to him personally, rather than to the pope in Rome. Around this time, Thomas Cromwell started referring to the pope as the bishop of Rome.

Thomas More was saddened by what was happening around him. He was a firm believer in

Rank and Privilege

English society had a very precise order during the time of King Henry VIII. At the top was the king or queen. Next came the great lords of the realm—men like the Duke of Norfolk and the Duke of Suffolk. Next in line came the great merchants and tradesmen of the realm. They generally lived in inner-city London. Next came the gentry, the lower-ranked nobles who lived in the countryside. Then came the yeoman farmers, men who owned their own land. Finally, there were the tenant farmers, people who rented land from others.

"Rank has its privileges," according to an old expression. This was certainly true in England during the time of King Henry VIII. The closer one was to the center of power, and the more friends one had at the center of power, the better one's chances for success. This is why the great nobles of England usually lived in London and spent much of their time at King Henry's court.

The further one lived from London and from the court, the dimmer one's chances of success. There were some exceptions to the rule, of course. Generally speaking, however, nearly everyone wanted to live close to London and have access to the royal court. Thomas More had been at the center of power for many years. He told his friends he was delighted to be leaving it.

the Roman Catholic Church. He did not wish to see King Henry, or any other king, take away powers that belonged only to the pope. In December 1532, Thomas More handed over his neck chain, the symbol of his office. He was Lord Chancellor no more.

Test Your Knowledge

1 Where was Thomas More in 1529, when a great
fire destroyed his barns and corn fields?
a. At home
b. In the service of the king
c. On a diplomatic mission to France
d. At a government meeting in London

2 What was the name for those people who did
not follow the teachings of the Catholic Church?
a. Heretics
b. Lunatics
c. Heathens
d. Sinners

3 Breaking with the Roman Catholic Church
would mean breaking with how many years
of established traditions?
a. 3,000
b. 5,000
c. 1,000
d. 2,000

4 Thomas Cromwell started referring to the pope as
a. the mayor of Rome.
b. the emperor of Rome.
c. the governor of Rome.
d. the bishop of Rome.

5 Thomas more was a firm believer in

a. the Roman Catholic Church.

b. the sanctity of marriage.

c. keeping his job at any cost.

d. all of the above.

ANSWERS: 1. b; 2. a; 3. c; 4. d; 5. a

A Prisoner
of Conscience

Thomas More was once again a private citizen. For the first time in about 15 years, he could retire to his family, his books, and his land in Chelsea. He was pleased with the change. He had grown weary of public service. True, he had grown wealthy in the service of King Henry VIII, enjoyed great power, and done some good things with that power, but now he could relax.

Thomas More was happy to return home. He had missed the regular contact with his family, which was now becoming very large. His three daughters were all married. Margaret had married William Roper. Cecily had married John Heron. Elizabeth had married Lord Dauncy. His son was also now married. John More had married one of his father's wards. There were seven grandchildren in the family already. Thomas More enjoyed teaching his grandchildren as much as he had enjoyed teaching his own children.

There were other matters to work on, as well. The house, land, and farm all required a good deal of management. Dame Alice More had done this for years, but now Thomas More was able to work with her. There were many reasons for Thomas More to be happy and content in his retirement, but he was not allowed to enjoy it.

King Henry VIII married Anne Boleyn just weeks after Thomas More resigned as Lord Chancellor. A few months after that, King Henry granted himself a divorce. He was probably the first person in history to do so. As supreme head of the new English Catholic Church, King Henry announced his own divorce from Queen Catherine. She was sent to live in a drafty, old castle, and she was forbidden from seeing her beloved daughter, Princess Mary.

In June 1533, King Henry VIII and Anne Boleyn solemnly proclaimed their new marriage to the world. There was a great festival in London to celebrate Anne Boleyn's being crowned as the new queen of England. Several of Thomas More's friends asked him to attend the new queen's coronation. Believing he needed money, they sent him enough to buy a new gown for the event, but Thomas More would not go. Even after three friends came to the house and asked him in person, he still would not go to the coronation of Anne Boleyn.

In part, More's refusal was due to the fact that he had always admired Queen Catherine. Even more important, however, was the fact that he believed the king's divorce and marriage both went against Roman Catholic law. What Thomas More did not expect was that, by not attending the queen's coronation, he was placing himself in peril. Thomas More should have known what was coming. He had

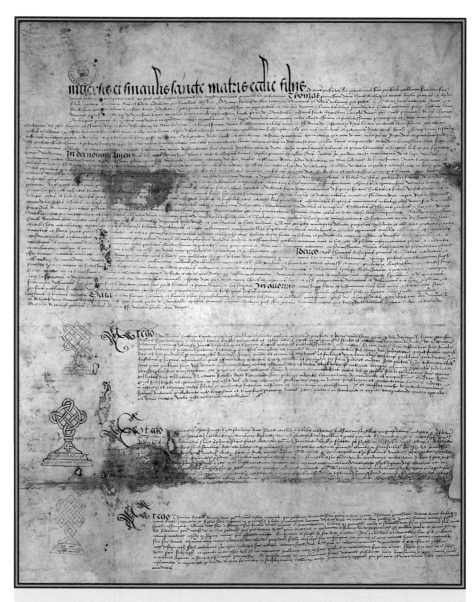

King Henry VIII was probably the first person in history to grant himself a divorce. Notification of the sentence of divorce between Henry VIII and Catherine of Aragon is shown here.

been around King Henry VIII long enough to know
that the king had a vengeful side. King Henry VIII
could never stand to be opposed by anyone.

Thomas More believed, or perhaps he hoped,
that his silence would serve as his protection. He
said nothing publicly against the divorce or the
new marriage. He made no comments about Anne

The Holy Maid of Kent

Elizabeth Barton, the Holy Maid of Kent, lived in
Kent, in the southeastern part of England. She
was a simple farm girl who began to have visions
around the age of 15. Her glorious visions foretold
her own recovery from a serious illness. Elizabeth
Barton went on to become a celebrity in Kent. She
was given a place to live in Canterbury, the holiest
site in England. Her visions were reported to crowds
and she became rather famous by the age of 20.

In the new world that King Henry VIII was
creating, religious experiences like those of
Elizabeth Barton were not welcome. She came
under suspicion for opposing the king's divorce and
new marriage. In fact, she predicted that he would
not keep his crown long if he married Anne Boleyn.

Boleyn or the coronation ceremony, but that was not good enough for King Henry VIII.

In 1533, Parliament passed a new law. It was called the Act in Restraint of Appeals. Under the provisions of the new law, English bishops and priests could no longer appeal to the pope in Rome to settle their disputes. They could only appeal to King Henry VIII.

In 1534, she and a group of her followers were burned at the stake.

Thomas More had met the Maid of Kent twice. He showed great respect for her and her visions, and Thomas Cromwell used this against him. Because Thomas More spent time with people who spoke out against the Act of Succession, logic said he must also be against the act. Today we call this guilt by association.

Thomas More and Elizabeth Barton were two very different people. Both of them died, however, as martyrs. The new secular society of the Renaissance would replace the religious society of the Middle Ages, but not soon enough to save Thomas More and Elizabeth Barton.

Next came the Act of Succession. Passed in 1534, the act declared the king as the supreme head of the new English Catholic Church. The act also declared that the king's former marriage to Catherine of Aragon was null and void. All of the king's subjects were required to swear an oath showing their support for the king, his new queen, and the Act of Succession.

Thomas More did not want to stand against King Henry. He knew the danger in that, but he could not, in good conscience, swear to the Act of Succession. Throughout his life, Thomas More had believed in the authority of the pope and the Roman Catholic Church. Now, in order to marry Anne Boleyn, King Henry had brought church and state together—a union that remains true in England even today.

In the last part of his life, Thomas More felt he had to stand up for his own conscience. He would not, could not, swear to the Act of Succession. For a while, it seemed as if Thomas More might have found a way out of the situation. He would not swear to the act, but neither would he speak against it.

Then, in the spring of 1534, Thomas More was called on by several English gentlemen. They required him to swear to the act, but he declined to do so. For a few days, Thomas More was kept as a "guest" of the bishop of London. When he still would not swear to the oath, he was confined to the Tower of London.

Thomas More described his circumstances in a letter to his daughter Margaret Roper:

> Our Lord be thanked, I am in good health of body, and in good quiet of mind: and of worldly things I no more desire than I have. I beseech him make you all merry in the hope of heaven. And such things as I somewhat longed to talk with you all, concerning the world to come, our Lord put them to your minds, as I trust he doth, and better too, by his Holy Spirit.[12]

Thomas More explained that he had no pen and was using a piece of charcoal to write the letter. He concluded:

> By your tender loving father, who in his poor prayers forgetteth none of you all, nor your babes, nor your nurses, nor your good husbands

shrewd wives, nor your father's shrewd wife
neither, nor our other friends. And thus fare
you heartily well for lack of paper. Thomas
More, Knight.[13]

The letter displayed why Thomas More was
beloved and admired by so many people. He had
a great ability to adapt to different circumstances
and the highs and lows of life. He did not despair
in the Tower of London. He almost seemed to
enjoy the challenge that had been thrust upon him.

Days and weeks passed, and Thomas More
received more paper and better pens for his writing.
He not only kept in touch with his family at Chelsea,
but also began to write a major new book. Published
long after his death, it was called *A Dialogue of
Comfort Against Tribulation.*

Thomas More certainly knew a lot about tribulation. After refusing to swear to the Act of Succession,
he lived under the threat of the rope, knife, or
executioner's block. King Henry VIII was not known
for his mercy toward those who opposed him.

In *A Dialogue of Comfort,* Thomas More never
mentioned King Henry VIII or the religious

The Act of Succession, passed in 1534, made King Henry VIII the supreme head of the new English Catholic Church. When Thomas More refused to swear to the act, he was imprisoned in the Tower of London. His cell is shown here.

changes that had brought about the new English Catholic Church. Instead, he set his new book in the kingdom of Hungary, just five or six years earlier. Hungary sits about 800 miles east of England, in the southeast section of Europe. The Hungarians had been invaded by the Ottoman Turks, first in 1521, and then again in 1526. Thomas More set his book in 1528. Much of the book was a dialogue between an old man named Anthony and a younger man named Vincent.

Thomas More wrote the book as if he were a Hungarian, writing about the events in his homeland. Although he did not live long enough to see the book published, his countrymen who read it could not help but find parallels between the book and the state of affairs in England in 1534.

In the book, the Turks are led by a vicious and cruel tyrant, Lord Suleiman. Though Thomas More never makes a direct comparison, one is inclined to think that Lord Suleiman is modeled after King Henry VIII. The book also served as an argument for Christian unity. According to the two men in the dialogue, Christian Europe could never be defeated as long as it was united, but, as we know, it was not united. Martin Luther had split the Catholic Church in two, and one might say that Henry VIII went even further, splitting it into three parts. On a deep level, *A Dialogue of Comfort* said that one should not depend on a world that changes too much. Only God and heaven are reliable, and a wise person puts his or her trust in them.

Thomas More was in need of comfort, for his situation was about to worsen. By the beginning of 1535, his writing tablets were taken away. He could no longer receive visits, even from his beloved daughter Margaret Roper. King Henry VIII was impatient. He wanted Thomas More to take the oath of the Act of Succession. Failing that, he wanted Thomas More to be tried for treason.

The trial of Thomas More began in May 1535. As a lawyer, Thomas More had attended many trials. He knew the law very well, but this time he was on the receiving end of the law and its punishments. There were very few protections for a person accused of treason in Thomas More's time. His was not a jury trial and, as the person accused of a crime, he had to prove his innocence, rather than being presumed innocent. From the start of the trial, Thomas More did not try to dispute the fact that he opposed the Act of Succession. Instead, he argued that his silence should be taken as quiet assent. This was a fine point of law. According to Thomas More, if a person did not state his objection, then his silence could be taken as assent. As complicated as the legal proceedings were, More's argument was the start of the idea that one could not be asked to incriminate oneself at trial.

The judges were having none of Thomas More's fine point of law. They knew "Sir Thomas," as they called him, and they were not going to be taken in by a legal trick. They continually pressed the point that, whether he said so or not, he opposed the Act of Succession.

One thing the judges used against More was his friendship with Elizabeth Barton, the Holy Maid of Kent. A young woman of about 20, she had religious visions and prophesies that said King Henry VIII would lose his throne if he married Anne Boleyn. Thomas More sidestepped the judges and the questions. Skillfully, he pointed out that he had never made any statements against the act.

Then a new witness, Richard Rich of Chelsea, came forward. A neighbor of Thomas More's, Richard Rich had visited More at the Tower of London about two months earlier. He declared that Sir Thomas had stated his objections to the Act of Succession during that visit. According to Richard Rich, the two men had a long conversation about the matter.

Thomas More took a swipe at Richard Rich, claiming everyone in Chelsea knew him as a gambler, a debtor, and a person of no importance. None of these accusations mattered. Richard Rich had made it easy for the judges to find Thomas More guilty.

The judges decreed that Thomas More should be hanged, drawn, and quartered, and that his body parts should be put in different places around the kingdom, as King Henry might see fit. Thomas More's last letter was sent from the Tower of London on July 5, 1535. He addressed it to his daughter Margaret Roper:

Our Lord bless you good daughter and your good husband and your little boy and all yours and all my children and all my godchildren and all our friends. Recommend me when you may to my good daughter Cecile, whom I beseech our Lord to comfort. . . . I send now unto my good daughter Clement her algorisme stone. . . . I pray you at time convenient recommend me to my good son John More. I liked well his natural fashion.[14]

The letter contained no words for Dame Alice More. Perhaps Thomas More had let her know of his fate by some other letter, which may have disappeared from history.

The execution was set for July 6, 1535. Thomas More, dressed in his best clothes, was taken to Tower Hill. A small crowd had gathered to watch. One woman called out that she had once been to court when Thomas More was the judge, and he had ruled against her. Thomas More called out that he remembered very well and, if the case were brought before him this day, the decision would be exactly the same.

Brought to the scaffold, Thomas More made one last joke, a last attempt to be cheerful. He asked one of the guards to help him climb up the scaffold and asked him to leave it to him to find his way down later.

The executioner, who wore a mask, begged for Thomas More's forgiveness. Thomas More granted it to him and the end came swiftly. There was only one blow of the axe.

King Henry VIII had changed the sentence at the last minute, so that Thomas More died a quick death from the executioner's axe. There was no hanging, drawing, or quartering. Even so, Thomas More's head was placed on a pole in the Tower of London, to show everyone what happened to traitors.

Test Your Knowledge

1 Thomas More was once again a private citizen for the first time in about how many years?

a. 17

b. 25

c. 15

d. 11

2 When Thomas More returned home, there were how many grandchildren in the family?

a. Ten

b. Seven

c. Eight

d. Six

3 What did the Act of Succession do?

a. Made the king the supreme ruler and head of the new English Catholic Church

b. Made the king the supreme ruler of all of Europe

c. Made the pope the supreme ruler and head of the new English Catholic Church

d. Prohibited the people from practicing Christianity

4   In the last part of his life, Thomas More
    felt he had to stand up for
    a. his religious beliefs.
    b. his marriage.
    c. his political career.
    d. his conscience.

5   In what year was Thomas More executed?
    a. 1535
    b. 1525
    c. 1555
    d. 1543

ANSWERS: 1. c; 2. b; 3. a; 4. d; 5. a

The Legacy of Thomas More

Right up until his death in 1535, Thomas More remained a man of faith. He held steadfastly to his strong religious beliefs and his faith in the Roman Catholic Church, resisting the religious changes of his time. We do not get to choose the time into which we are born. People come into the world and have to adjust to what they find. Thomas More entered a world full of pageantry and mystery. The late Middle Ages were full of symbolic gestures, and Thomas More became a master at performing many of them.

By the time Thomas More was 30, the Renaissance had taken hold in Northern Europe. Painters, sculptors, and writers adjusted to the changing times. They created paintings, sculpted statues, and wrote books that showed the new age of realism. Renaissance artists wanted to portray the world and human beings as they were, rather than as people thought they should be. Hans Holbein's famous sketch of Thomas More and his family shows this new Renaissance realism.

For a time, in his 30s, it appeared that Thomas More would be a major Renaissance artist. He was neither a painter nor a sculptor, but he was a writer of great talent. His *Utopia* was a masterful blend of wishful thinking and prophecy. Today, he almost seems to have predicted aspects of modern life.

In the end, Thomas More turned away from being a Renaissance artist and used his art—his

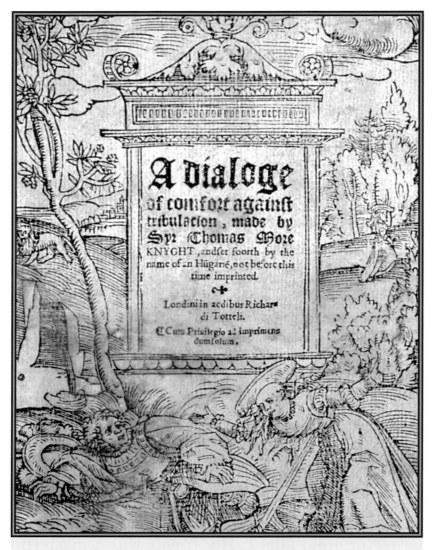

Thomas More's *A Dialoge of Comfort Against Tribulation* was published long after his death. While it never mentioned King Henry VIII or the religious changes that brought about the new English Catholic Church, readers did find parallels between the book and the state of affairs in England in 1534.

writing—in defense of the old order. Perhaps the fierce attack of Martin Luther on the Roman Catholic Church galvanized More's resolve, or perhaps More simply grew older and more conservative.

Thomas More served both Cardinal Thomas Wolsey and King Henry VIII. More was fond of saying he never sought these high positions, that they simply came to him, sometimes against his own desires. Regardless of how he attained prestige, rise he did, in a spectacular, though brief, climb to power.

The crisis of King Henry's Great Matter was the beginning of the end for Thomas More. Even Thomas Wolsey had not found an answer to that one. Only Thomas Cromwell came up with the ingenious and radical solution of breaking away from the Roman Catholic Church and creating the English Catholic Church.

As we know, Thomas More became a prisoner of his own conscience. He could not, in good conscience, support King Henry's divorce or his new marriage. The results were fatal for Thomas More. He died as a martyr to the cause of the Roman Catholic Church of the Middle Ages.

Thomas More was recognized as a martyr right away, but he did not become a saint of the Roman Catholic Church until 1935, some 400 years after his death. He was a man of great skill, navigating his way through the treacherous times of King Henry

A Man for All Seasons

One of the finest movies of the 1960s was *A Man for All Seasons*. Peter O'Toole played the lead role of Thomas More. The movie portrayed the lively and loving household of Thomas More at Chelsea. Viewers saw Thomas More with his wife and family, and got a glimpse of the kind of man he was. He was portrayed as devout, upright, and fearful of what might happen to him, but committed nonetheless.

One of the most memorable scenes occurred when King Henry VIII and a large group of courtiers rowed up the Thames to visit Thomas More. The visit was unexpected and Dame Alice More quickly put food on the fire to be ready. Meanwhile, the king and Thomas More walked in the beautiful gardens.

King Henry VIII put on his most charming face. He smiled at Thomas More, put his arm around

VIII. He was a fine family man, a devoted husband, a father, and a grandfather to his large family. He was a writer of superior skill. Finally, he was a man of firm conscience. He was not threatened by the fears that made others cower. Once, when he was threatened

him, and asked him as kindly as possible, "Will you agree to the new marriage with Anne Boleyn?" Thomas More did not say no. He did not say yes, either. Instead he praised the king, saying he was a great and good man, and that his will would be done in this matter. The king left, as charming as ever, but unsatisfied.

Weeks later, the marriage of King Henry and Anne Boleyn was celebrated. At one point in the celebration, King Henry saw someone in the corner. He thought it was Thomas More. Delighted and overcome with joy, the king rushed to the corner calling out, "Thomas!" Then the person turns, and we see it is not Thomas More. The king is bitterly disappointed. *A Man for All Seasons* blends fact with fiction, while still doing an admirable job of presenting Thomas More in a realistic light.

King Henry VIII's Great Matter marked the beginning of the end for Thomas More. More became a prisoner of King Henry VIII in the Tower of London, but he also became a prisoner of his own conscience. More's arrest is shown here.

by Thomas Cromwell and others with the possibility of torture, Thomas More replied, "These threats are for little children, Master Secretary, not for me!" As long as words are used, as long as religious debates are held, and as long as people debate the great questions of life and death, Thomas More will be remembered.

Test Your Knowledge

1 The late Middle Ages were full of
   a. mysterious occurrences.
   b. symbolic gestures.
   c. religious persecution.
   d. spiritual awakenings.

2 What marked the beginning of the end for Thomas More?
   a. The king's Great Matter
   b. His marriage to Dame Alice
   c. His appointment as Lord Chancellor
   d. His desire to advance in his career

3 Thomas More died as a martyr to what?
   a. The middle-class citizens of London
   b. King Henry VIII
   c. The government of London
   d. The Roman Catholic Church

4 How many years after his death was Thomas More made a saint of the Roman Catholic Church?
   a. 200
   b. 350
   c. 400
   d. 500

5 In addition to being a family man and a man of conscience, Thomas More was

a. a writer of superior skill.

b. a musician.

c. a gourmet cook.

d. an accomplished financial advisor.

ANSWERS: 1. b; 2. a; 3. d; 4. c; 5. a

1478   Thomas More is born in London.

1484   Thomas More begins school in London.

1485   King Richard III is killed at the Battle of Bosworth Field; Henry Tudor is crowned as King Henry VII.

1491   Prince Henry is born; he will become King Henry VIII.

1499   Thomas More meets Desiderius Erasmus for the first time.

1500   Start of the sixteenth century.

1505   Thomas More is married to Jane Colt.

1505   Their first child is born.

1521   King Henry VIII publishes a book against Martin Luther

1478   Thomas More is born in London

1516   Thomas More's *Utopia* is published

1478

1505   Thomas More marries Jane Colt

1511   Thomas More's wife dies; he marries Alice Middleton; Desiderius Erasmus lives for a while with the More family; he writes *In Praise of Folly*

1509 King Henry VII dies and King Henry VIII ascends to the throne; Thomas More becomes undersecretary to the treasurer of London.

1511 Thomas More's wife dies; he marries Alice Middleton; Desiderius Erasmus lives for a while with the More family; he writes *In Praise of Folly.*

1516 Thomas More's *Utopia* is published.

1517 Thomas More goes on a diplomatic assignment in Calais; Martin Luther issues his 95 Theses against indulgences.

1526 The King's
Great Matter
begins

1935 Thomas More is
made a saint of the
Catholic Church

1535 Thomas More
is executed

1935

1532 Thomas
More resigns as
Lord Chancellor

1533 The Act
of Succession
is enacted

1520   The Field of the Cloth of Gold is held outside of Calais, France.

1521   King Henry VIII publishes a book against Martin Luther.

1523   Thomas More serves as leader of the House of Commons.

1526   The king's Great Matter begins.

1529   Thomas Cromwell helps in the divorce proceedings of King Henry VIII.

1529   Thomas More becomes Lord Chancellor of England.

1532   Thomas More resigns as Lord Chancellor.

1533   The Act of Succession is enacted.

1533   King Henry VIII marries Anne Boleyn.

1534   Thomas More is taken to the Tower of London.

1535   Thomas More is executed.

1935   Thomas More is made a saint of the Catholic Church.

NOTES

CHAPTER 1
A Family Portrait
1. Richard Marius, *Thomas More.*
   New York: Alfred A. Knopf,
   1984, p. 224.
2. Ibid.
3. Ibid., p. 225.
4. Ibid.
5. Ibid.

CHAPTER 2
Father and Son
6. Desiderius Erasmus, *The Collected
   Works of Erasmus.* Toronto,
   Canada: University of Toronto
   Press, 1969, vol. 85, p. 27.
7. Ibid., p. 39.

CHAPTER 3
A Rising Star
8. Leicester Bradner and Charles
   Arthur Lynch, eds., *The Latin
   Epigrams of Thomas More.* Chicago:
   University of Chicago Press,
   1953, pp. 138–139.

CHAPTER 5
The King's Servant
9. Elizabeth Frances Rogers, ed.,
   *The Correspondence of Sir Thomas
   More.* Princeton, NJ: Princeton
   University Press, 1947,
   p. 21.

CHAPTER 8
Thomas More, Lord Chancellor
10. Rogers, *The Correspondence
    of Sir Thomas More*, p. 422.
11. Ibid., p. 423.

CHAPTER 9
A Prisoner of Conscience
12. W.E. Campbell, ed., *The Last
    Letters of Blessed Thomas More.*
    London: The Manresa Press,
    1924, p. 44.
13. Ibid., pp. 44–45.
14. Rogers, *The Correspondence
    of Sir Thomas More*,
    pp. 563–564.

Ackroyd, Peter. *Thomas More.* New York: Nan A. Talese/Doubleday, 1998.

Bradner, Leicester and Charles Arthur Lynch, eds. *The Latin Epigrams of Thomas More.* Chicago: University of Chicago Press, 1953.

Campbell, W.E., ed. *The Last Letters of Blessed Thomas More.* London: The Manresa Press, 1824.

Manning, Alice. *The Household of Thomas More.* New York: E.P. Dutton, 1906.

Marius, Richard. *Thomas More: A Biography.* Boston: Harvard University Press, 1998.

Rogers, Elizabeth Frances, ed. *The Correspondence of Sir Thomas More.* Princeton, NJ: Princeton University Press, 1947.

Routh, E.M.G. *Sir Thomas More and his Friends, 1477–1535.* Oxford, England: Oxford University Press, 1934.

Ackroyd, Peter. *The Life of Thomas More.* New York: Nan A. Talese/ Doubleday, 1998.

Marius, Richard. *Thomas More: A Biography.* Boston: Harvard University Press, 1998.

Murphy, Anne. *Thomas More.* Liguori, MO: Liguori Publications, 1997.

Roper, William. *Life of Sir Thomas More.* Springfield, IL: Templegate Publishers, 1980.

Websites

The Last Letter of Sir Thomas More, 1535
http://englishhistory.net/tudor/primore.html

Modern History Sourcebook: The Life of Sir Thomas More
http://www.fordham.edu/halsall/mod/16Croper-more.html

Modern History Sourcebook: Sir Thomas More, *Utopia*, 1516
http://www.fordham.edu/halsall/mod/thomasmore-utopia.html

page:

3: © Bridgeman Library
8: © Scala/Art Resource, NY
15: © HIP/Art Resource, NY
21: © HIP/Art Resource, NY
31: © Erich Lessing/Art Resource, NY
41: © Snark/Art Resource, NY
46: © Bridgeman Library
54: © Magdalen College, Oxford/Bridgeman Library
59: © Réunion des Musées Nationaux/Art Resource, NY
65: © Bridgeman Library
68: © Uffizi, Italy/Bridgeman Library

76: © Erich Lessing/Art Resource, NY
81: © Birmingham Museums and Art Gallery/Bridgeman Library
90: © Philip Mould, Historical Portraits Ltd, London, UK/Bridgeman Library
92: © Weston Park Foundation, UK/Bridgeman Library
101: © HIP/Art Resource, NY
107: © Scala/Art Resource, NY
118: © Guildhall Library/ Bridgeman Library
122: © Musee de Blois/ Bridgeman Library

Cover: © Scala/Art Resource, NY

Samuel Willard Crompton lives in the Berkshire Hills of western Massachusetts. He is the author or editor of many books, most of them in history and biography. He first became interested in Thomas More when he saw *A Man for All Seasons*. Mr. Crompton was raised a Roman Catholic and is now a spiritual seeker. He teaches history at Holyoke Community College.